# MUSIC FROM THE MOTION PICTURE SOUNDTRACK

ISBN 978-1-4584-0304-9

HAL•LEONARD®
CORPORATION
7777 W. BLUEMOUND RD. P.O. BOX 13819 MILWAUKEE, WI 53213

Visit Hal Leonard Online at
**www.halleonard.com**

# REAL IN RIO
## (Capture)

Music by JOHN POWELL, SERGIO MENDES
and CARLINHOS BROWN
Lyrics by SIEDAH GARRETT

**Fast Samba**

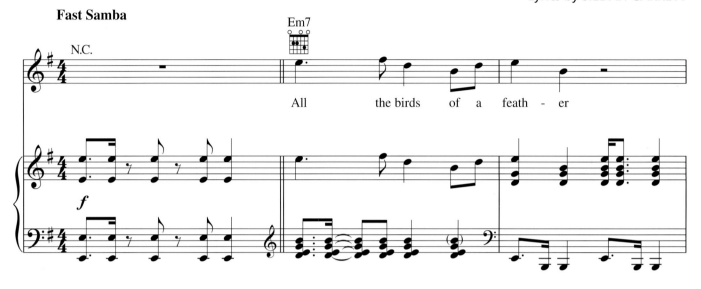

All the birds of a feath-er

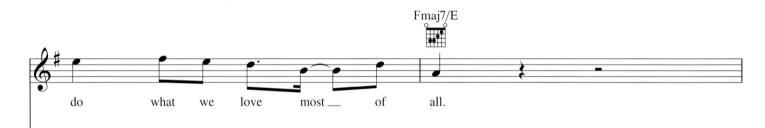

do what we love most ___ of all.

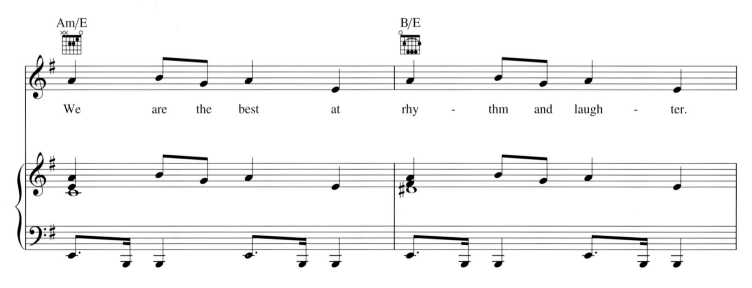

We are the best at rhy-thm and laugh-ter.

Ma - gic___ can hap - pen___ for re - al in

Ri - o, all by it - self.___

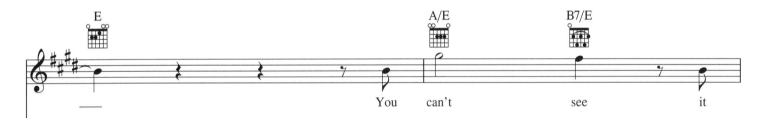

You can't see it

com - ing; you can't find it an - y - where

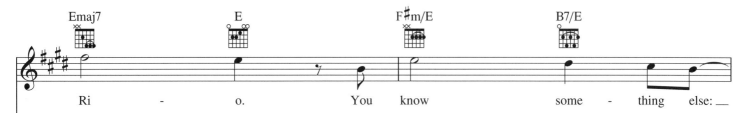

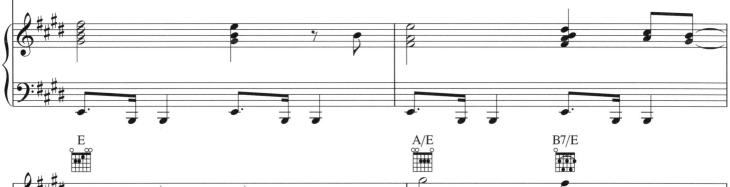

# LET ME TAKE YOU TO RIO
## (Blu's Arrival)

Music by CARLINHOS BROWN,
MIKAEL MUTTI and ESTHER DEAN
Lyrics by CARLINHOS BROWN
and ESTHER DEAN

(Ri - o, Ri - o, Ri - o, yeah, Ri - o, Ri - o, Rio.)

Let me take you to Ri - o, Ri - o, fly on the o - cean like an ea - gle, ea - gle.

And we can chill in my ga - ze - bo, ga - ze - bo, oh, _____ na, na, na.

To Coda

# MAS QUE NADA

Words and Music by
JORGE BEN

**Moderate Samba, in 2**

pois o sam-ba es-ta a-ni-ma - do o que

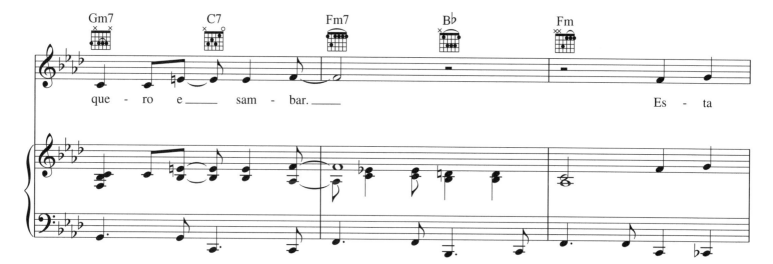

que - ro e \_\_\_\_ sam-bar. \_\_\_\_ Es - ta

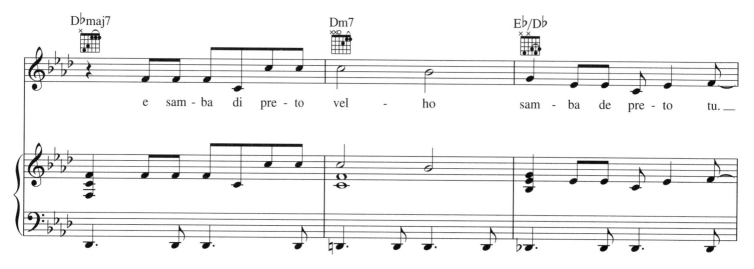

sam - ba \_\_\_ que e mis - to de ma-ra-ca-tu \_\_\_\_

e sam-ba di pre-to vel - ho sam-ba de pre-to tu. \_\_

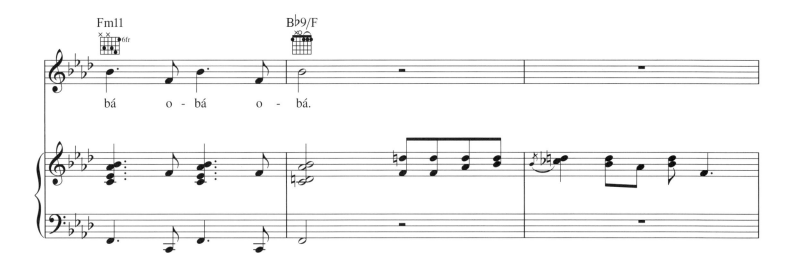

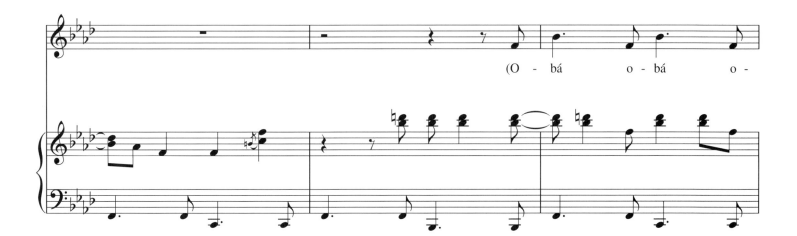

bá.) (O -

bá o - bá o - bá.)

(O - bá o - bá o - bá.)

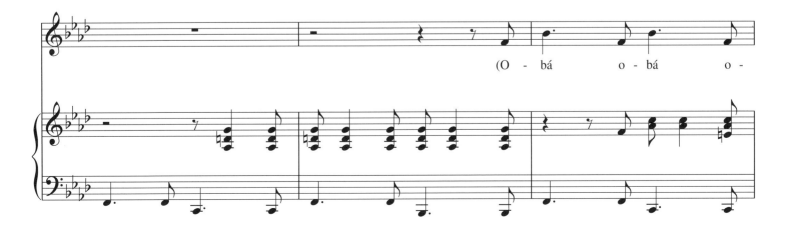

(O - bá o - bá o -

bá.)   (O -

bá   o - bá   o - bá.)

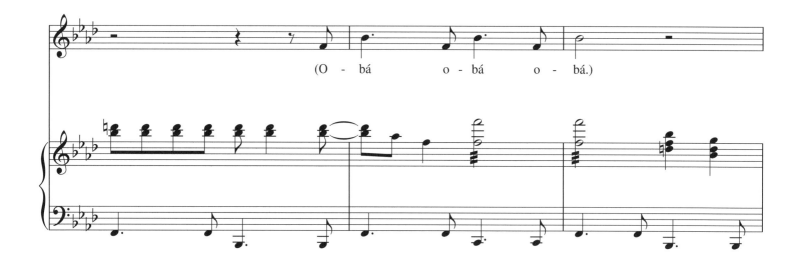

(O - bá   o - bá   o - bá.)

# HOT WINGS
## (I Wanna Party)

Words and Music by
WILLIAM ADAMS

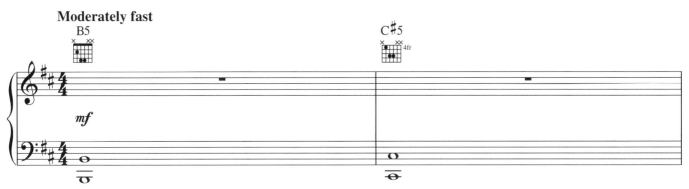

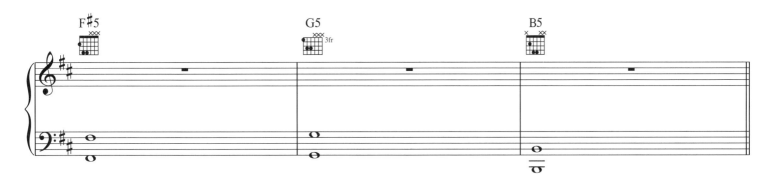

24

*Squawk like a bird.

# PRETTY BIRD

Music by JEMAINE CLEMENT
and JOHN POWELL
Lyrics by JEMAINE CLEMENT,
YONI BRENNER and MIKE REISS

**Moderately**

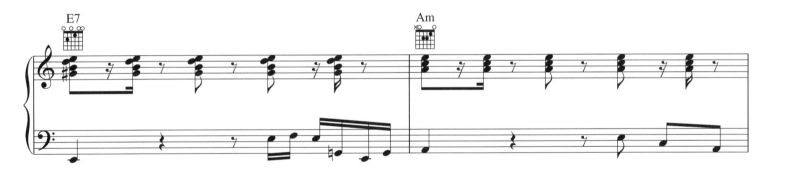

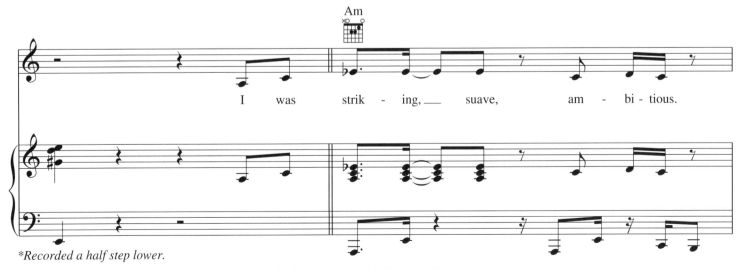

I was strik - ing, ___ suave, am - bi - tious.

*Recorded a half step lower.

Coah - ca - ca - ca - ra - ca - ra, co - oh - oh - ah!)

go - ing to do: I'm go - ing to make you... *Spoken: Shut up now!*

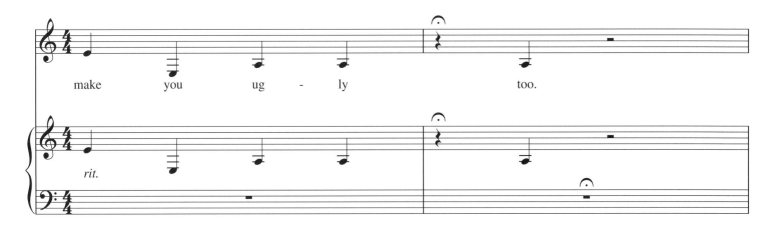

*Shut up!*      *It's just me.*      I will

make you ug - ly too.

**Tempo I**

Ah - ha - ha - ha - ha - ha - ha - ha - ha - ha - ha - aagh!    Ha - ha - ha - ha - ha - ha, ah - haa!

# FLY LOVE

Music by CARLINHOS BROWN
Lyrics by SIEDAH GARRETT

**Moderate Bossa Nova**

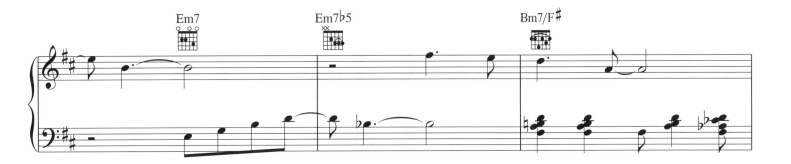

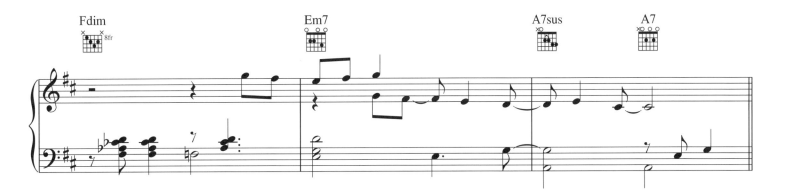

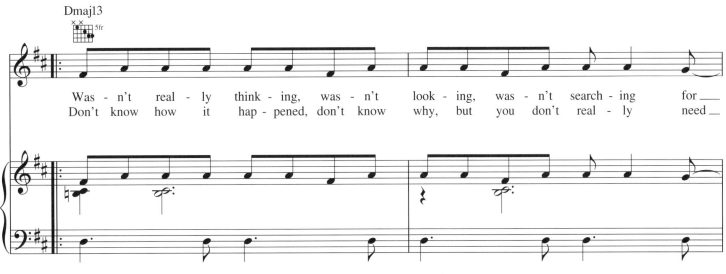

Was - n't real - ly think - ing, was - n't look - ing, was - n't search - ing for ___

Don't know how it hap - pened, don't know why, but you don't real - ly need ___

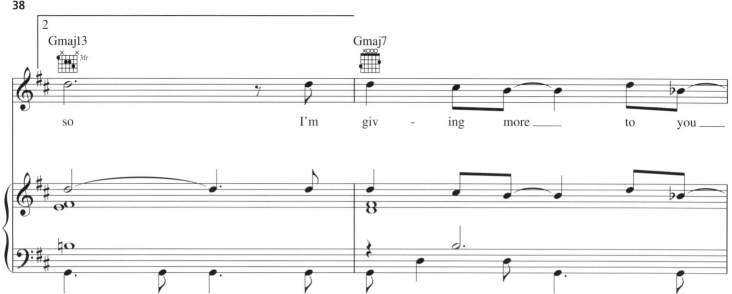

so I'm giv - ing more ___ to you ___

___ than I thought I could do. ___

# TELLING THE WORLD

Words and Music by TAIO CRUZ
and ALAN KASIRYE

for, _____ a rea-son for light. _____

_____ Oh ay oh, oh ay

oh, _____ ah. (He yay ___ ee yay.) ___ Oh ay

oh, oh ay oh _____ ah. (He yay ___ ee yay. ___

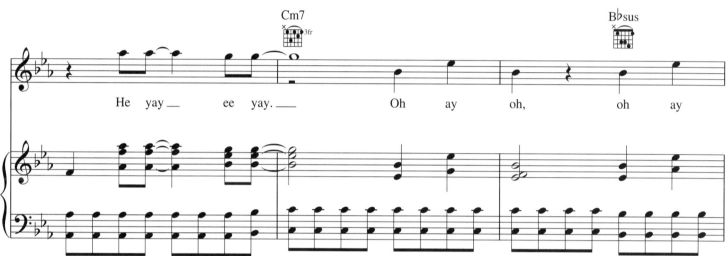

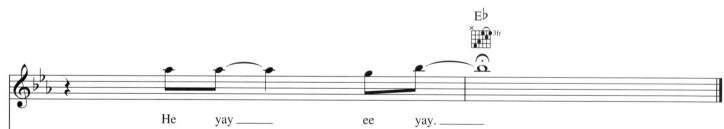

# TAKE YOU TO RIO

Music by TOR ERIK HERMANSEN
and MIKKEL STORLEER ERIKSEN
Lyrics by ESTHER DEAN

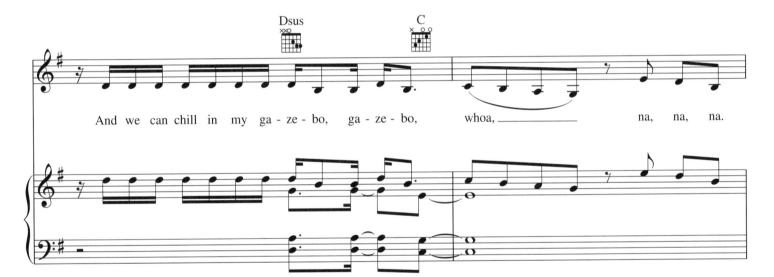

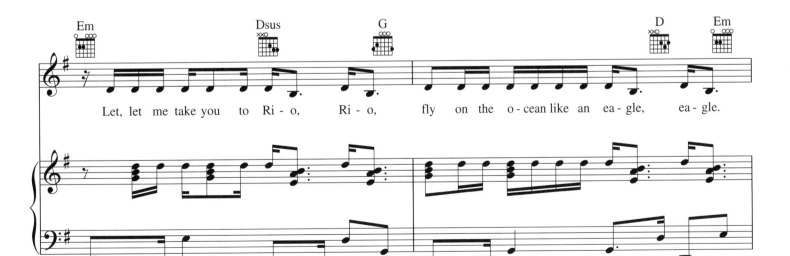

And we can chill in my ga - ze - bo, ga - ze - bo, oh, oh, _____ na, na, na.

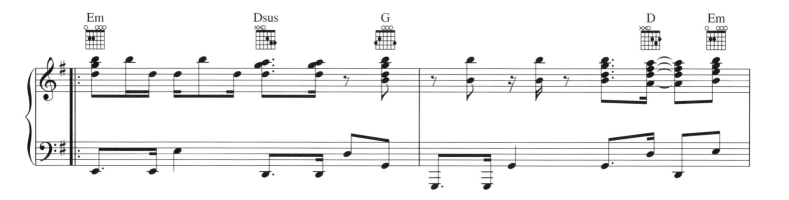

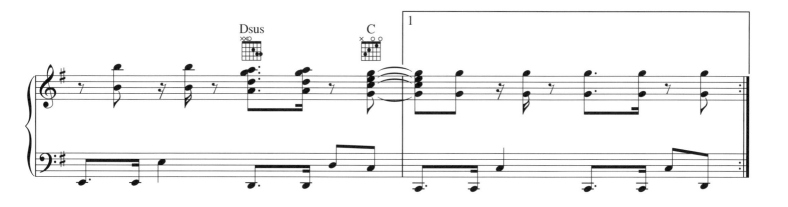

# VALSA CARIOCA

Words and Music by
SERGIO MENDES

**Moderate Waltz**

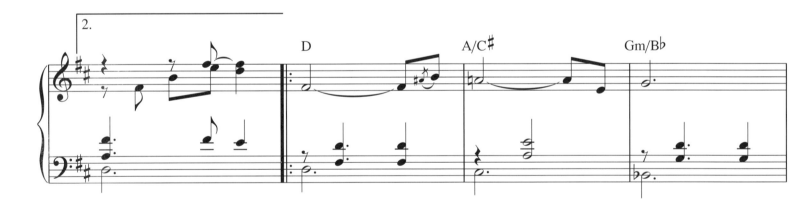

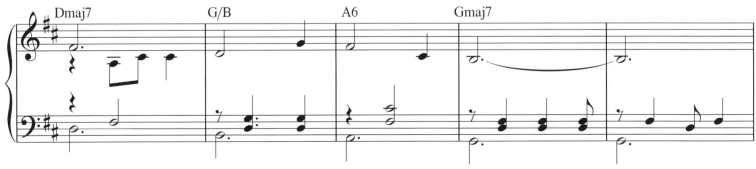

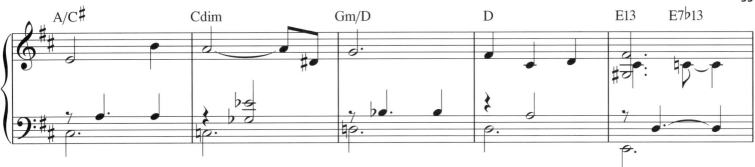

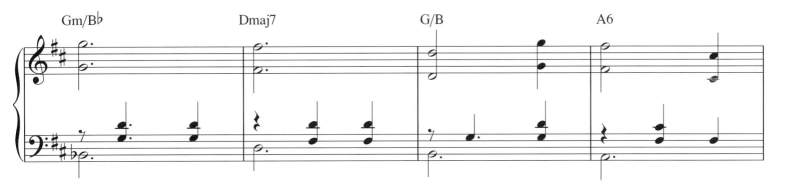

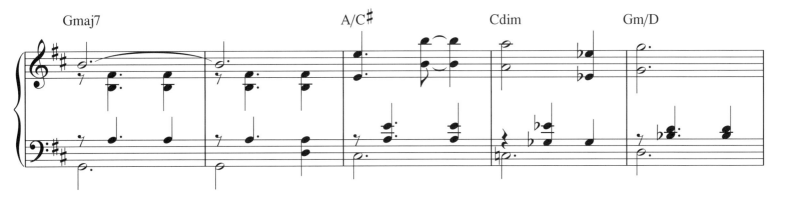

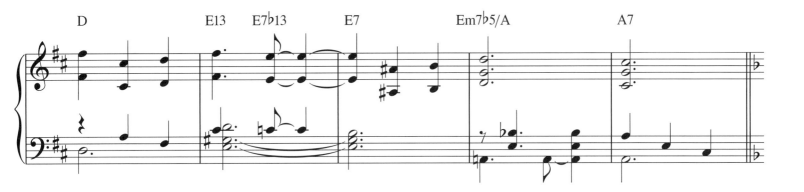

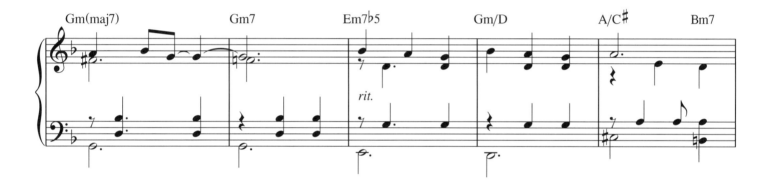

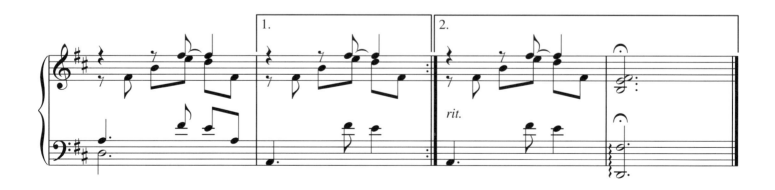